Rough Guides

25 Ultimate experiences

World Food

Make the most of your time on Earth

ROUGH GUIDES

25 YEARS 1982–2007

NEW YORK • LONDON • DELHI

Contents

Introduction

EXPERIENCES have always been at the heart of the Rough Guide concept. A group of us began writing the books **25 years ago** (hence this celebratory mini series) and wanted to share the kind of travels we had been doing ourselves. It seems bizarre to recall that in the early 1980s, travel was very much a minority pursuit. Sure, there was a lot of tourism around, and that was reflected in the guidebooks in print, which traipsed around the established sights with scarcely a backward look at the local population and their life. We wanted to change all that: to put a country or a city's popular culture centre stage, to highlight the clubs where you could hear local music, drink with people you hadn't come on holiday with, watch the local football, join in with the festivals. And of course we wanted to push travel a bit further, inspire readers with the confidence and knowledge to break away from established routes, to find pleasure and excitement in remote islands, or desert routes, or mountain treks, or in street culture.

Twenty-five years on, that thinking seems pretty obvious: we all want to experience something real about a destination, and to seek out travel's **ultimate experiences**. Which is exactly where these **25 books** come in. They are not in any sense a new series of guidebooks. We're happy with the series that we already have in print. Instead, the **25s** are a collection of ideas, enthusiasms and inspirations: a selection of the very best things to see or do – and not just before you die, but now. Each selection is gold dust. That's the brief to our writers: there is no room here for the average, no space fillers. Pick any one of our selections and you will enrich your travelling life.

But first of all, take the time to browse. Grab a half dozen of these books and let the ideas percolate … and then begin making your plans.

Mark Ellingham
Founder & Series Editor, Rough Guides

25

Ultimate

experiences

World

Food

1 Picking crabs *in* Maryland

Hands stained red with Old Bay seasoning, fingers so slick with crab fat you can hardly clutch your beer, maybe a few stray bits of crab shell stuck in your hair or to your cheek – that's the sort of dishevelment you should be aiming for at a Maryland crab feast.

"Picking" hard-shell steamed blue crabs is a sport Marylanders attack with gusto from May to October – though anyone will tell you that the heaviest, juiciest number-one "jimmies" are available only near the end of the summer. That's when the most popular crab restaurants up and down the bay have lines out the door, and every other backyard in Baltimore seems to ring with the sound of wood mallets smacking on crab legs.

It's simplicity itself: a bushel or two of crabs in the steamer with some beer and lashings of spicy Old Bay, and yesterday's newspaper laid out on a big picnic table, along with a few rolls of paper towels. What else? Only more beer (cold this time), some corn on the cob, a hot dish or two . . . nothing to distract from the main attraction.

Then it's down to business. The process starts with yanking what can only be described as an easy-open pull tab on the crab's under-shell. From there, dig out the yellowish fat called "mustard", as well as the gills, then snap the hard-back shell in half and proceed to scoop out the sweet, succulent flesh. Soon you'll be whacking the claws just so with a wooden mallet and gouging the meat out with a knife.

It's easier than it sounds, and the crabmeat is certainly a powerful motivator for thorough picking (and fast learning). In the process, you can't help but marvel at man's cleverness when it comes to eating critters with the prickliest of defences. But maybe that's just the beer talking.

a bushel or two
of crabs in the steamer
with some beer …

need to know

A crab feast is best in a backyard or church basement, but Annapolis's venerable **Cantler's Riverside Inn**, 458 Forest Beach Rd (℡410/757-1467, Ⓦwww.cantlers.com), or **Kelly's**, 2108 Eastern Ave (℡410/327-2312) or **Costas Inn**, 4100 Northpoint Blvd (℡410/477-1975), both in Baltimore, will do the trick.

need to know

The best smörgåsbords are served on Saturday and Sunday mornings at **The Grand Hotel Stockholm,** S Blasieholmshamnen (℡08 679 35 00; 380kr), and **Ulriksdals Wärdshus**, **Slottspark** (℡08 85 08 15; 300kr), ten minues north of Stockholm in Solna. More extravagant is **Operakällaren**, Operahuset at Karl XII's torg (℡08 676 58 01; 920kr), which in the month leading up to Christmas puts on an elaborate holiday buffet known as a *julbord*.

Smörgåsbord

Offhand, how many different ways can you think of to prepare herring or salmon? The two fish are staples of the smörgåsbord, and at last count, there are well over 120 varieties being used in restaurants and kitchens across Sweden.

The Swedish smörgåsbord (literally "buttered table") is a massive all-you-can-eat buffet where you can sample almost anything under the midnight sun, from heaping plates of fish and seafood – pickled, curried, fried or cured – to a dizzying assortment of eggs, breads, cheeses, salads, patés, terrines and cold cuts, even delicacies such as smoked reindeer and caviar.

You're best off arriving early and on an empty stomach. Just don't pile everything high onto your plate at once –remember that the tradition is as much celebratory social ritual as it is one of consumption. That means cleansing your palate first with a shot of ice-cold aquavit (caraway-flavoured schnapps), then drinking beer throughout – which as it happens goes especially well with herring, no matter the preparation.

Plan to attack your food in three separate stages – cold fish, cold meats and warm dishes – as it's generally not kosher to mix fish and meat dishes on the same plate. Layer some slices of herring onto a bit of rye bread, and side it with a boiled potato, before moving on to smoked or roasted salmon, jellied eel or roe. Follow this with any number of cold meats such as liver paté, cured ham and oven-baked chicken. Then try a hot item or two – Swedish meatballs, wild mushroom soup, perhaps *Janssons frestelse* ("Jansson's temptation"), a rich casserole of crispy matchstick potatoes, anchovies and onion baked in a sweet cream. Wind down with a plate of cheese, crackers and crisp Wasa bread and, if you can still move, fruit salad, pastries or berry-filled pies for dessert, capped by a cup of piping hot coffee. Then feel free to pass out.

3

Mixing sand and spice on Ko Samui

Ko Samui is perhaps an unlikely spot to learn the art of Thai cooking. Given the choice between spending endless hours lapping up rays on a speck of sand, palms and waterfalls in the Gulf of Thailand and arming oneself with a sharp cleaver to take on a mound of raw pork and fiery chilies hardly seems worthy of debate — especially when the best plate of food you're likely to have in your life costs about a buck at the local market.

Yet the packed schedule at the **Samui Institute of Thai Culinary Arts** suggests otherwise. The school focuses on central Thai food, considered the classic style among the country's four regional cuisines with its coconut-milk curries and flavourful balance of hot, sour, salty and sweet. The classes begin with a discussion of the ingredients (and how to substitute for those hard to find outside of Southeast Asia), work up to hands-on wok skills and end with a feast of your own making, an array of stir fries, curries and soups.

Walk into the school's unassuming shophouse just off Samui's Chaweng Beach and you may wonder whether you've been shanghaied into a tropical Iron Chef gone awry. A sea of tiny bowls bursting with cumin seeds, tamarind, coriander root, galangal and shrimp paste lie scattered across the prep tables, and you've got a little more than two hours to whip up three dishes. But before panic sets in, the lead chef calmly explains how to chiffonade a kaffir lime leaf, and soon enough, you're grinding out a proper chili paste in a mortar and pestle with the steady hand of a market lady who's been at it for fifty years. It can't be this easy, can it? Chop a few more chilles, toss in an extra dash of fish sauce, swirl the wok and – *aroy mak* – you've just duplicated that *tom yum kai* (spicy shrimp soup) you saw at the market. So what if it cost a few dollars more?

need to know

A 2hr 30min class at SITCA, on Soi Colibri (☎077 413172, ⓦwww.sitca.net), costs B1600 (about $40); classes are held twice daily.

Visiting the home of pizza in Italy

4

Making something this elemental is a precise art, and it's all in the base – toppings are kept plain in Italy, especially in Naples, where pizza was invented. Here even cheese is sometimes considered a luxury. The base must be thrown around within an inch of its life by the pizza-maker or *piazzaiolo*, until it is light and airy, rolled thin, spread with its topping, and then thrown into a wood-fired brick oven until it just begins to burn and blister – a pizza that doesn't have at least a few traces of carbon just isn't worth eating.

A simple dish of bread dough spread with tomatoes and mozzarella cheese cooked in the hottest oven you can muster, pizza is probably the most widespread – and most misunderstood – fast food in the world. Given that they serve it just about everywhere, it's also the least exotic, and certainly one of the most variable. Some say that pizza is like sex: even when it's bad it's still pretty good. Truth is, it can be terrible. But in Italy, the home of pizza, it can be sublime.

Neapolitan pizzas, thin-based but typically with a thick chewy crust, are unusually venerated: even northern Italians, who hate everything from the South, acknowledge that these are the best. Roman pizzas are no slouch either, always served crispy-thin, and, as in Naples, with the simplest of toppings – although specifically Roman ingredients like zucchini flowers may be added. Rome is also the home of pizza *bianca* – no topping really, just sprinkled with herbs and drizzled with oil – and fantastic by the slice (*al taglio*).

You can of course get versions of the above from your supermarket, or perhaps order up a pie from the nearest delivery spot and never leave the comfort of your own home. But without making the trip to Italy you won't know what it's like to eat the real thing – and there are so many great places to do it: some of the country's best pizzerias are the most basic, with limited menus and rough-and-ready service. One thing to remember: although you can of course get pizza any time, proper pizzerias only open in the evening. Expecting to have one for lunch will mark you out as a hopeless tourist!

need to know

The perfect Roman pizza: Ai Marmi, Viale di Trastevere 53–59.
The perfect Neapolitan pizza: Di Matteo, Via dei Tribunali 94.

5

The best snack known to man in America's food capital

The long tick-list is staring you in the face. Overstuffed pastrami sandwich at *Katz's Deli*. Foot-long Nathan's hot dog out at Coney Island. Eight-course tasting menu costing a couple of hundred of dollars at *Jean Georges*, or *Per Se*, or *Gramercy Tavern*. Soup dumplings costing next to nothing at any number of Chinatown holes-in-the-wall. Brunch at an impossibly cute West Village café. The bistro burger, washed down with a $2 McSorley's, at *Corner Bistro*. Then again, this is why you came to New York.

But there's one grave omission, one that may well be the quintessential New York dish. And it's got everything to do with the water. At least that's what they say: a crusty yet chewy New York bagel, first boiled in that water before being baked, is just better because of it. Whether that comes near to the truth, no snack is more a symbol of the city than a bagel with cream cheese, piled high with lox (smoked salmon), and a few slices of tomato and red onion, perhaps some capers for effect. You can find bagels nearly everywhere, of course, and many claim to be the best, but no one does it quite like **Russ and Daughters.**

It's not a restaurant or diner but an "appetizing" store, family-owned to boot, and they've spent four generations brining, baking, whipping and generally perfecting the art of righteous Jewish food. It's mostly known for its smoked fish, and you can't go wrong with any of their salmon offerings (or their whitefish or sable, for that matter). But the salty belly lox, cured rather than smoked, may be most toothsome of all their fishy delights. Lay it over their own homemade, soul-satisfying cream cheese, smeared on a garlic bagel, also made in-house, and you've got the best accompaniment to a cup of coffee and the *New York Times* known to man.

need to know
Russ and Daughters is on Manhattan's Lower East Side, at 179 E Houston St (℡212/475-4880, ⊛www.russanddaughters.com). A bagel with lox and cream cheese runs about $8.

6
Mopping up a Moroccan
Tajine

need to know

A Moroccan tajine can cost anything
from 20 to 200 dirhams ($2–23/£1–
12). For about the same price, you
can buy the cooking pot – which is
traditionally plain earthenware, but
can also come in very pretty ceramic
versions.

Robert Carrier, one of the twentieth century's most influential food writers, rated Moroccan cuisine as second only to that of France. Which is perhaps a little hyperbolic, for, outside of the grandest kitchens, Moroccan cooking is decidedly simple, with only a half dozen or so dishes popping up on most local menus. But no matter where you are in the country, from a top restaurant to the humblest roadside stall, there is one dish you can depend upon: the tajine.

A tajine is basically a stew. It is steam-cooked in an earthenware dish (also called a tajine) with a fancifully conical lid – and most often prepared over a charcoal fire. That means slow-cooking, with flavours locked in and meat that falls from the bone.

What goes in depends on what's available. At a market stall, it's quite possible that your cook will take the order then go off to buy the ingredients – right down to a fresh chicken. But a number of combinations have achieved classic and ubiquitous status: *mrouzia* (lamb or mutton with prunes and almonds – and lots of honey) and *mqualli* (chicken with olives and pickled lemons), for example. On the coast, you might be offered a fish tajine, too, frequently red snapper or swordfish. And tajines can taste almost as good with just vegetables: artichokes, tomatoes, potatoes, peppers, olives, and again those pickled lemons, which you see in tall jars in every shop and market stall. The herbs and spices, too, are crucial: cinnamon, ginger, garlic and a pinch of the mysterious *ras al-hanut*, the "best in shop" spice selection any Moroccan stall can prepare for you.

There's no need for a knife or fork. Tajines are served in the dish in which they are cooked, and then scooped and mopped up – using your right hand, of course – with delicious Moroccan flat bread. Perfect for sharing.

And when you're through, don't forget to sit back and enjoy the customary three tiny glasses of super-sweet mint tea.

Seeing stars in
SAN SEBASTIÁN

Many who make their way to the genteel resort of San Sebastián, in Spain's Basque region, have one thing on their mind: food. Within the country, País Vasco – as the Basque area is known – has always been recognized as serving Spain's finest cuisine, but it's only relatively recently that word has got out beyond it's borders. The city in fact boasts the most impressive per capita concentration of Michelin stars in the world, a reflection of its deep-rooted gastronomic tradition finally coming of age. And while feisty newcomers like *Mugaritz* make international headlines, Juan Mari Arzak is widely regarded as the one

who kicked it all off back in the 1970s.

Long the holder of three of those cherished stars, his *Arzak* restaurant remains the parlour-informal, family-friendly temple of audacious yet almost always recognizably Basque food; a meal here is a thrilling affair. Deftly incorporating line-caught fruits of the Cantabrian sea, the flora and fauna of the Basque countryside and flavours from further afield (a sister branch operates in Mexico City), Arzak and his daughter Elena are as likely to cook with smoked chocolate, cardamom, dry ice-assisted sauces and ash-charred vinaigrette as the signature

GAMBAS PLANC
LANGOSTINOS
CALAMARES FRI
ANCHOAS FRIT
TORTILLA BACA

truffles and foie gras. Bold, subversive takes on Spanish classics – strawberry gazpacho anyone? – confound and exhilarate while longstanding favourites like truffle-distilled poached egg are so flawlessly presented you'll hesitate to slice into them. And despite the gourmet prices, the ratio of gregarious locals to foodie pilgrims means there's little scope for snobbery.

Still, if cost is an issue, you can experience San Sebastián's epicurean passions by way of a *txikiteo*, the Basque version of a tapas crawl. Taste your way through a succession of tempting *pintxos* – their name for the baroque miniatures on offer – at hearteningly unpretentious bars like *Txepetxa, Ganbara* and *La Cuchara de San Telmo*, in the *parte vieja* (old town). Marinated anchovies with sea urchin roe, papaya or spider crab salad, tumblers of viscous garlic broth and earthy wild musroom confit come with a tiny price tag – just a few euros – but with lasting reward.

need to know

Arzak, Avda Alcalde Elosegui 273 ☎943 278 465, ⓦwww. arzak.es; tasting menu costs €125. You can find excellent *pintxos* bars scattered throughout the old town.

8 Filling up on little eats in Taiwan

Crowded alleyways, blaring scooter horns and a mix of Mandopop and Nokia tunes may not sound like an appealing night out, but there's a reason why Taiwan's night markets pack people in – some of the best food in Asia.

The Taiwanese love food so much, they've perfected what's known in Chinese as "little eats" (*xiaochi*), tasty snacks served in small portions – think Chinese take-out meets tapas. The places most associated with *xiaochi* are night markets held all over the island; most get going in the evening and don't typically close till after midnight. Each stall has a speciality, a "little eat" it likes to promote as food fit for an emperor. But royal lineage is unimportant, as is language: just point, pay and stuff it down.

At **Shilin**, Taipei's best and biggest night market, a typical evening starts with a few warm-up laps, perhaps grabbing a couple of appetizers along the way: a sugar-glazed strawberry, fried pancake with egg, or succulent Shilin sausage served with raw garlic and eaten with a cocktail stick. Suitably inspired, it's time for a little more chopstick work: many stalls own a cluster of plastic tables and chairs where you can slurp and munch while seated. Classic dishes include slippery oyster omelettes covered in luscious red sauce, and addictive *lu rou fan*, juicy stewed pork on rice. Still hungry? Try some celebrated regional specialties: *danzi mian* from Tainan (noodles with pork, egg and shrimp), or deep-fried meatballs from Changhua.

Serious connoisseurs – or more likely those with adventurous palates – can opt for the really scary stuff. Most infamous are *chou doufu*, cooked in pig fat and better known as stinky tofu, the smell of which sickens newcomers but the taste of which is sublime (the fried, crispy outer layer perfectly balances the fluffy tofu underneath), and *lu wei*, a savoury blend of animal guts, simmered in broth, and often eaten cold. Try this, washed down with a cold Taiwan beer, and you're certain to win the respect of the incredulous Taiwanese sitting next to you.

need to know

Shilin Night Market in Taipei is opposite Jiantan MRT station, and is open daily. Most dishes cost NT$25–50 (under US$2).

9 Beefeater's paradise: the Argentinean parrilla

Argentineans rich or poor tend to base their high-protein diets around beef; they eat more of it per capita than any other people on earth. Who can blame them? Succulent, juicy and flavourful, Argentine beef has a distinct, refined taste, redolent of the perfect pasture that the cattle graze upon – the incredibly fertile pampa, an emerald green carpet radiating out for hundreds of miles around Buenos Aires.

The beef's flavour is expertly brought out in its preparation. The traditional – in fact, practically the only – method is on a *parrilla*, a barbecue using wood (or occasionally charcoal, but certainly never gas). Almost sacred to Argentineans, the *parrilla* is a custom that has its roots in gaucho (cowboy) culture: the fire is lit on Sundays, holidays, after football matches, pretty much at any excuse. In the countryside, ranch hands

spread the embers along the ground; in the town, chefs use a metal pit. A grill is hung above and the food lined up – fat chorizo sausages and rounds of melting provolone cheese to start, followed by tasty *asado* ribs and, finally, huge slabs of steak.

The meat is of such quality that there's no need to drown it in sauces – the parrillero (cook) will lightly season it and offer up some chimichurri to add zip. Made of herbs, garlic and peppers in oil, chimichurri was purportedly invented by a Scottish (or Irish) gaucho named Jimmy McCurry (or Curry), who mixed the only ingredients he had to hand to spice up his diet. Vegetables are an afterthought, mostly restricted to fries and salad – the only essential accompaniments to a parrilla are bread and a bottle of rich, red Argentinean Malbec.

need to know

The best parrillas are found outside of Buenos Aires, closer to the source. Stay on an *estancia* (ranch), such as El Ombú (@www.estanciaelombu.com), to enjoy beef reared on site, or seek out family-run parrillas found in pretty much every countryside town. Alternatively, upmarket city restaurants (like Cabaña Las Lilas, Av Alicia M de Justo 516, in the capital's converted docks area) offer premium cuts of meat in more sophisticated surroundings.

10

Trying every TACO in Mexico

It may very well be possible to eat your way around all 761,606 square miles of Mexico without having the same taco twice. The stars of Mexican curbside cuisine, taco vendors dish up a huge array of intense flavours, all wrapped up in a deceptively bland-looking tortilla or two. Regional differences start here, with the northern states favouring chewy flour tortillas and the rest of the country staying loyal to the native maize, in the form of earthy corn tortillas.

From there, it's a free-for-all. Yucatecans love their bright-orange sweet-sour shredded pork (*cochinita pibil*) and deep-fried shrimp, while folks in Michoacan line up to pick their favourite part of the pig for *tacos de carnitas*. Steamed, succulent *barbacoa*, whether goat, pork or beef, is popular at breakfast, but nighttime is the right time for the ubiquitous *tacos al*

Worried about hygiene? Don't be. You get to see your meal cooked up right in front of you, which also presents the best opportunity for the sidewalk chef to show off his skills and tantalize passersby with the smell of sizzling meat.

Once the *taquero* has fried, grilled or boiled your chosen filling, he expertly dices it into bite-size pieces, tilts it into a soft tortilla and tops it with chopped onion and cilantro. Then it's up to you to pile on salsa, a squeeze of lime, maybe some sliced radish. It's no coincidence that often the colours on top – red salsa, green cilantro, white onion – are the same as those on the Mexican flag.

need to know

You'll find the best, busiest taco vendors in front of bus stations and on plazas where service taxis and *vans* gather. Expect to pay between M$10 and M$15 for one, though they are often sold two or three to an order (*un orden*).

pastor, chili-spiced pork and pineapple roasted on the same spinning skewer used in the Middle East for shawarma (hence the other name for this distinctly Mexican concoction, *tacos arabes*). If you tire of meat, try a filling of *huitlacoche* – a slick black corn fungus that tastes distinctly of bacon – or even a tortilla full of fried grasshoppers, enjoyed in Oaxaca.

27

11
Toasting bad weather
IN THE SCOTTISH HIGHLANDS

need to know

Speyside is Scotland's principal whisky-making area. The **Malt Whisky Trail** (@www.maltwhiskytrail.com) points you in the direction of eight distilleries offering guided tours, including the Glenlivet and the Glenfiddich; plenty more distilleries around Scotland and on some of the islands, notably Islay, open their doors to visitors. Still, the best places to sample single malts may be Scottish pubs and hotels.

First, be glad that it rains so much in Scotland. Without the rain the rivers here wouldn't run – the Livet, the Fiddich, the Spey. Without the rain the glens wouldn't be green and the barley wouldn't grow tall and plump.

Be glad it's damp here in Scotland. Peat needs a few centuries sitting in a bog to come out right. Then a breeze, and a wee bit o' sun, to dry it. You burn it, with that delicious reek – the aroma – to dry the malted barley. Earth, wind and fire.

And be glad it's cold here in Scotland. Whisky was being made in these hills for centuries before refrigeration. Cool water to condense the spirit. And if you're going to leave liquid sitting around in wooden barrels for ten or more years you don't want it too warm. The evaporation – the angels' share – is bad enough. Still, it makes the idea of "taking the air" in Speyside rather more appealing.

And if it weren't cold and wet and damp you wouldn't appreciate being beside that roaring fire and feeling the taste for something to warm the cockles. Here's a heavy glass for that dram, that measure. How much? More than a splash, not quite a full pour. Look at the colour of it: old gold.

Taste it with your nose first; a whisky expert is called a "noser" rather than a "taster". Single malts have all sorts of smells and subtleties and flavours: grass, biscuits, vanilla, some sweet dried fruit, a bit of peat smoke. Drinking it is just the final act.

Aye, with a wee splash of water. The spirit overpowers your tastebuds otherwise. A drop, to soften it, unlock the flavours. Not sacrilege – the secret. **Water.**

Is it still raining?
Let me pour you another.

12

Assembling a picnic

from

Sarlat market

Ready for lunch? Given the range and quality of foodstuffs available from small producers in France, there's no better solution than to buy your own picnic at a local market – and no better place to do it than Sarlat.

This medieval town tucked in a fold of hills on the edge of the Dordogne valley hosts one of the biggest and best markets in southwest France.

For centuries people have been flocking to Sarlat market, where the banter is just as likely to be in local dialect as in French. The stalls under their jaunty parasols groan with local produce, from a rainbow array of seasonal fruit and vegetables to home-baked cakes and the famous foie gras, the fattened liver of goose or duck.

Let your nose guide you first to the charcuterie van selling aromatic pork or venison sausage and locally cured ham. There are terrines of *rillettes*, a coarse duck or goose pâté, and melt-in-the-mouth foie gras, sometimes laced with truffles, the

"black diamonds of Périgord". Next up is the farmer tempting customers with slivers of cheese. The regional speciality is *cabécou*, a small, flat medallion of goat's cheese, but you'll also find creamy ewes-milk cheese from the Pyrenees and Salers and Bleu d'Auvergne from the Massif Central.

A few tomatoes – still sun-warm and packed with flavour – and a cucumber make a quick salad. Then you need bread. Traditionalists will opt for a crusty *pain de campagne*, but wholemeal baguettes and rye or seed-speckled granary breads are just as prevalent. While you're at it, ask for some wedges of walnut cake or *pastis*, a lip-smacking apple tart topped with crinkled pastry and more than a hint of armagnac.

Last stop is the fruit stall. Any season proves bountiful, from the first cherries of spring through summer strawberries to autumn's apples, pears and fat chasselas grapes. Now tear yourself away to find a sunny spot on the banks of the Dordogne – not forgetting the wine and corkscrew of course.

Bon appétit!

need to know

Sarlat is on the River Dordogne, 170km east of Bordeaux. Its main food market takes place on Saturday mornings from 8am to 1pm in and around the main central square, place de la Liberté.

31

13

Beijing duck

Beijing 1985: Mao has been dead for nine years but China is still reeling from the effects of his restrictive policies, which have held the country's economy back at almost pre-industrial levels. People shuffle around dispiritedly in blue Mao suits, bicycles outnumber cars about a thousand to one, the air is heavy with the smell of charcoal burning in braziers and the most modern buildings are functional, grey, communist-inspired concrete blocks. The only shops selling anything other than daily necessities are the "Friendship Stores", full of imported luxuries such as televisions and the locals that dream about earning enough money to own one. Restaurants serving anything other than bland, uninspiring food are extremely thin on the ground. With one very notable exception:

the Quanjude Roast Duck restaurant,

founded in 1864 and recently resurrected after being closed down during the Maoist era. Enter most restaurants in China and you're herded into a special "foreigners' only" section out of sight of indigenous diners (for whose benefit it isn't clear), but not here: for Chinese and foreigners alike it's a free-for-all, where only the quick and strong get fed. The dining hall is so crammed with tables that there's barely room to fit the chairs in, and that's a big problem because all available room – absolutely every inch – is occupied by salivating customers hovering like vultures beside each chair, waiting for the person sitting down to finish their meal and begin to get up. The ensuing moments of hand-to-hand combat, as three people try to occupy the half-empty seat, end with the victor knowing that they are about to enjoy a cholesterol-laden feast. First comes the duck's skin, crispy brown and aromatic; next the juicy meat, carefully sliced and eaten with spring onion slivers, all wrapped inside a thin pancake; and lastly, a soup made from duck bones and innards. And all for ¥12 – less than two dollars for a night's entertainment.

need to know

Quanjude Roast Duck restaurant, 32 Qianmen Dajie, Beijing ☎010/6701 1379. Customers no longer need to fight for a seat; reservations are advisable. A whole duck – enough for two – now costs ¥170.

The great African meat feast

need to know

Standard practice at meat bars is to go to the kitchen and order by weight direct from the butcher's hook or out of the fridge. If you're treating your hosts, ordering beef on the rib (a kilo per person) is a pretty sure way to please them. Carnivore, the ultimate nyama choma bar, is Nairobi's best-known and biggest restaurant, on Longata Road. (☎020/605933-7, ⓦwww.carnivore.co.ke).

Ask any expat East African what food they miss most and they'll tell you nyama choma. In the Gambia, it's known as afra; and in South Africa it's what you have at a braai. All over the continent, roast or grilled meat is the heart of any big meal and, whenever possible, it is the meal. A meat feast is also the only occasion in Africa when you'll find men doing the cooking – charring hunks of bloody flesh clearly answering a visceral male need that every king of the cookout would admit.

Most people don't eat meat often, subsisting on a simple starch dish for their regular meal of the day, so it's perhaps not surprising that when the occasion demands or provides a banquet, meat is the main fare. In Kenya or Tanzania, unless you're lucky enough to be invited to a wedding or funeral, you'll go to a purpose-built nyama choma bar, where flowing beer and loud music are the standard accompaniments, with greens and ugali (a stiff corn porridge, like grits) optional. The choice is usually between goat and beef, with game meat such as impala, zebra or ostrich available at fancier places. If you select one of these, usually with an all-you-can-eat price tag equivalent to about a week's average wages, you should cannily resist the early offerings of soup, bread and sausages, leaving space for the main events.

After roasting, your meat is brought to your table on a wooden platter, chopped up to bite-size with a sharp knife, and served with a small pile of spiced salt and a hot sauce of tomato, onion, lime and chilies. You eat with your fingers, of course. You'll need a good appetite, strong jaws and plenty of time – to wait for your chosen roast, to chew and digest, to pick your teeth while downing a few more beers and to honour the dance requests that inevitably come your way, no matter how full you might feel.

15

Gorging on
chocolates
in Belgium

need to know

Godiva, Place du Grand Sablon 47–48; **Pierre Marcolini**, rue des Minimes 1; **Wittamer**, Place du Grand Sablon 12; **Planète Chocolate**, rue du Lombard 24.

The Mayans may have invented chocolate long ago, but Belgium is its world headquarters, and nowhere more so than Brussels, whose temples to the art of the brown stuff are second to none. It's not just a touristy thing, although within the vicinity of the Grande-Place you could be forgiven for thinking so. Chocolate is massively popular in Belgium, and even the smallest town has at least a couple of chocolate shops; in fact, the country has 2000 all told, and produces 172,000 tonnes of chocolate every year. You may think that this would make for a nation of obese lardcakes, especially as Belgium's other favourite thing is beer (not even mentioning the country's obsession with *pommes frites*). However, whatever your doctor may tell you, chocolate in moderation is quite healthy. It's full of nutrition, reduces cholesterol and is easily digested. Some claim it's an aphrodisiac as well.

So what are you waiting for? Everyone has their favourite chocolatier – some swear by **Neuhaus**, while others rely on good old **Leonidas**, which has a shop on every corner in Brussels – but **Godiva** is perhaps the best-known Belgian name, formed in the early 1900s by Joseph Draps, one of whose ancestors now runs a chocolate museum on the Grande-Place. Once you've checked that out (and gobbled down a few free samples), make for the elegant Place du Grand Sablon, with not only a Godiva outlet, but also the stylish shop of **Pierre Marcolini**, who produces some of best chocs in the city, if not the world. **Wittamer**, also on Place du Grand Sablon, don't just do chocolates, and in fact you can sip coffee and munch on a chocolate-covered choux pastry at its rather nice café; you're probably best off saving that big box of Wittamer's delicious pralines for later ... though trying just a few now surely can't hurt. If you're not feeling queasy by this point, stop at **Planète Chocolate**, on rue du Lombard, where you can find the city's most exotic and adventurous flavours – pepper, rose, various kinds of tea – as well as watch the chocolate-making process in action, followed by (what else?) the obligatory tasting. Moderation be damned.

Downing CAIPIROINHAS in RIO DE JANEIRO

What could be simpler than a caipirinha? Made with just cachaça a rum-like spirit distilled from fermented sugarcane juice), fresh lime, sugar and ce, the caipirinha (literally 'little peasant girl") is served up at nearly every bar and restaurant in Brazil. Neither nsipidly sweet nor jarringly alcoholic, it's one of the easiest and most pleasant cocktails to drink.

need to know

Academia da Cachaça, Rua Conde de Bernadote 26, Leblon, in Rio de Janeiro (daily noon to 2am; ☎21/2529-2680, ⊚www.academiadacachaca.com.br).

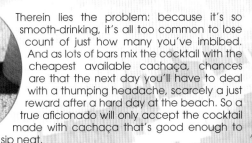

Therein lies the problem: because it's so smooth-drinking, it's all too common to lose count of just how many you've imbibed. And as lots of bars mix the cocktail with the cheapest available cachaça, chances are that the next day you'll have to deal with a thumping headache, scarcely a just reward after a hard day at the beach. So a true aficionado will only accept the cocktail made with cachaça that's good enough to sip neat.

There's no better place to find that than at Rio de Janeiro's **Academia da Cachaça**. Opened in 1985, when Brazil's aspirant whisky-drinking middle class tended to dismiss cachaça as the drink of the poor, the Academia has about a hundred varieties on offer, and the bar's friendly owners and staff enjoy nothing more than offering tasting hints to their customers.

As you enter you may well wonder what all the fuss is about. The green and yellow Brazilian-flag themed decor is utterly unremarkable and the music inaudible. But the shelves on the walls of the tiny bar, lined with a bewildering selection of bottles, remind you why you've come.

The caipirinhas are everything one might hope for, with just the right balance of alcohol, tang and sweetness. After one or two, you may even feel ready to forego the sugar, lime and ice and start downing shots. Choosing a label is easy: if you don't listen to the house recommendations, the regulars around you will intervene to suggest their personal favourites. The spirit inspires debates, not unlike those over the finest single malt whiskies. The perfection of the caipirinha, on the other hand, is undebatable.

17 The ritual of a kaisek

Kaiseki-ryori, Japanese haute-cuisine, was developed as an accompaniment to the tea ceremony; it has the same sense of ritual, meticulous attention to detail and exquisite artistry, all of which combine for a sublime sensory – if rather pricey – experience.

At a *kaiseki* restaurant the atmosphere is just as important as the food. Ideally, it will be in a traditional, wood-framed building. Kimono-clad waiting staff show you to a table set out on rice-straw *tatami* mats. A hanging scroll and a perfectly balanced flower arrangement, both chosen to reflect the season, enhance the air of cultural refinement. You look out on one of those wonderful Japanese gardens with not a leaf or pebble out of place.

The food fits the occasion and setting. A full *kaiseki* meal usually consists of ten to twenty small dishes, perhaps succulent slivers of raw fish with fiery wasabi relish, a few simmered vegetables, silky smooth tofu, toothsome pickled items, tempura as light as air. Only the freshest ingredients are used to create a flawless array of seasonal delicacies designed to complement each other in every way – taste, aroma, texture, visual appeal.

No less care goes into selecting the serving dishes. Lacquerware, hand-painted ceramics, natural bamboo and rustic earthenware both offset their contents and present a harmonious whole. It's all exceedingly subtle and full of cultural references, but don't worry – anyone can appreciate the sheer craftsmanship and the hours of preparation that have gone into the feast before you.

meal in Japan

It seems almost a crime to disturb the dramatic effect, but it would be an equal crime not to taste as much as possible. There isn't any particular order to diving in, just try to savour each delectable mouthful. The only firm rule is that rice and soup come last, as a filler - should you have any room to spare. And even in these august surroundings, it's perfectly acceptable to slurp your noodles.

need to know

In Tokyo, try **Kakiden**, 3-37-11 Shinjuku (☎03/3352-5121) or Kisso, 5-17-1 Roppongi (☎03/3582-4191). In Kyoto, there's **Hyotei**, Nanzen-ji (☎075/771-4116) and **Nakamura-ro**, 509 Gion-machi minami-gawa (☎075/561-0016). Expect to pay around ¥10,000 per person for dinner and ¥5000 for a mini-*kaiseki* lunch. Reservations are essential.

18 Searching for the perfect oyster on

Isla Margarita

Oysters provide a great source of inspiration for a food-driven odyssey. You can travel far and wide looking for the freshest, finest specimen; once discovered, you might consume it on the half-shell, or fried up in a po-boy sandwich, or perhaps as part of a shrimp and oyster omelette – a South Korean favourite.

Consider first what they are: sensitive little creatures that thrive in unpolluted areas, where fresh water and sea water mix and where temperatures aren't too hot in summer or too freezing in winter. In short, relatively unspoilt and often unusually attractive coastal spots. So you'll not only enjoy the goods when you arrive, you may find a picture-perfect setting too.

These spots lie in a band across the globe, taking in wild oysters from the fjords of Norway and South Africa lagoon oysters, as well as European oysters plantations in Loch Fynne (Scotland), Whitstable (England) and the 350-plus oyster farms on the Arcachon Basin, in France. But for our money, there's no cooler crustacean than mangrove oysters, and no more inspiring location in which to consume them than the coconut grove-lined beaches of Isla Margarita, Venezuela.

These bivalves, who call the roots of the red mangrove home, are much smaller than other oysters – typically measuring no more than 4cm across – so knocking back a couple dozen briny, salty-sweet ones for lunch (raw, of course, with a dash of citrus – the purist's choice), mandatory frosty Polar beer in hand, is no problem at all. While you're lazing on the beach, you only need to corral a vendor: armed with just a small blunt knife, a bag full of limes, a jar of fiery cocktail sauce and a plastic bucket full of lagoon water and mangrove oysters, these traders dispense a little bit of paradise.

need to know

The popular beaches of Playa El Agua or Playa Puerto Cruz, which together straddle the northern tip of Isla Margarita, are regularly patrolled by oyster vendors. A dozen oysters should cost around US$5.

Lunching on Creole cuisine in
New Orleans

New Orleans is a gourmand's town, and its restaurants are far more than places to eat. These are social hubs and ports in a storm – sometimes literally, in the case of the French Quarter kitchens that stayed open post-Katrina, dishing out red beans and rice to the stubborn souls who refused to abandon their beloved city. Above all, they are where New Orleans comes to celebrate itself, in all its quirky, battered beauty. And no restaurant is more quintessentially New Orleans than Galatoire's, the grande dame of local Creole cuisine.

Lunch, particularly on Friday and Sunday, is the meal of choice; set aside an entire afternoon. Reservations aren't taken for the downstairs room (the place to be), so you'll need to come early and wait in line. In true New Orleans fashion, this bastion of haute Creole style sits on the city's bawdiest stretch, Bourbon Street. Picking your way through the morning-after remnants of a Bourbon Saturday night – plastic cups floating in pools of fetid liquid, a distinctive miasma of drains and stale booze and rotting magnolias – brings you to a display worthy of a Tennessee Williams play. Seersucker-clad powerbrokers puff on fat cigars, dangling dainty Southern belles on their arms; immaculately coiffed women greet each other with loud cries of "dawlin'!" Inside – or downstairs at least – it's like time has stood still: brass ceiling fans whir overhead, giant old mirrors reflect the lights cast by Art Nouveau lamps, and black-jacketed waiters, who have worked here forever, crack wise with their favourite diners.

It's the same century-old menu, too: basically French, pepped up with the herbs and spices of Spain, Africa and the West Indies. Lump crabmeat and plump oysters come with creamy French sauces or a piquant rémoulade, a blend of tomato, onion, Creole mustard, horseradish and herbs; side dishes might be featherlight soufflé potatoes or fried eggplant. To end with a kick, order a steaming tureen of potent *café brûlot* – jet-black java heated with brandy, orange peel and spices – prepared tableside with all the ceremony of a religious ritual.

need to know

Galatoire's is at 209 Bourbon St (Tues–Sat 11.30am–9pm, Sun noon–9pm; ☎504/525-2021, ⊛www.galatoires.com). Jackets required for men after 5pm and all day Sunday.

20

snake every which way in

Hanoi

When the man bringing your meal to the table is missing most of his fingers and the main ingredient is not only still alive but also long and writhing and – hang on, is that a cobra?

need to know

Hanoi's most famous snake restaurants are in the suburb of Le Mat, including the reliable **Quoc Trieu** (☎04/827 2988). Prices start at around 100,000VND per head excluding drinks. Be sure to fix the price beforehand.

– well, that's when you know this is no ordinary dining experience. Eating at one of Hanoi's snake restaurants is as much a theatrical performance as a meal out.

The decor is way over the top. From a grungy side-street you enter a world of exuberant woodwork with mother-of-pearl inlay glowing in the lantern light. Bonsai plants are scattered artfully while off to the side glass jars containing snake wine hint at what's to come.

When everyone's settled, the snake handler – he with very few fingers – presents the menu. He kicks off with cobra, the most expensive item on the menu (and a choice photo-op), then runs through the other options, all very much alive and hissing. Traditionally, your chosen snake is killed in front of you, though it will be dispatched off-stage if you ask. The guest of honour (lucky you?) then gets to eat the still-beating heart. The Vietnamese say it contains a stimulant and that the meat is an aphrodisiac. The jury's out on both counts, however, because of the copious amounts of alcohol everyone consumes. By way of an aperitif you get two small glasses of rice wine, one blood red, the other an almost fluorescent, bile-ish green ... which is exactly what they are.

Things get decidedly more palatable as the meal starts to arrive. In a matter of minutes your snake has been transformed into all manner of tasty dishes: snake soup, spring rolls, dumplings, filets, even crispy-fried snake skin. Absolutely nothing is wasted. It's washed down with more rice wine, or beer if you'd rather, and to round things off, fresh fruit and green tea – no snake sorbet forthcoming.

No one takes cheese as seriously as the Swiss.
Elsewhere, cheese is one element within a more complex meal. In Switzerland, cheese is the meal – and fondue is the classic cheese feast.

Pick a cold night and gather some friends: fondue is a sociable event, designed to ward off the Alpine chill with hot comfort food, warming alcohol and good company. No Swiss would dream of tackling one alone.

In French, *fondre* means "to melt": fondue essentially comprises a pot of molten cheese that is brought to the table and kept bubbling over a tiny burner. To eat it, you spear a little cube of bread or chunk of potato with a long fork, swirl it through the cheese, twirl off the trailing ends and pop it into your mouth.

Those are the basics. But you'll find there's a whole ritual surrounding fondue consumption that most Swiss take alarmingly seriously. To start with, no one can agree on ingredients: the classic style is a *moitié-moitié*, or "half-and-half" – a mixture of Gruyère and Emmental – but many folk insist on nutty Vacherin Fribourgeois playing a part, and hardy types chuck in a block of stinking Appenzeller. Then there's the issue of what kind of alcohol to glug into the pot: kirsch (cherry spirit) is common, but French-speaking Swiss prefer white wine, while German speakers from the Lake Constance orchards stick firmly to cider.

Once that's decided and the pot is bubbling, everyone drinks a toast, the Swiss way: with direct eye contact as you say the other person's name – no mumbling or general clinking allowed! Then give your bread a good vigorous spin through the cheese (it helps stop the mixture separating), but lose it off your fork and the drinks are on you.

If the whole thing sounds like a recipe for a stomachache, you'd be spot-on: imagine roughly 250g (half a pound) of molten cheese solidifying inside you. There's a reason for the traditional *coup de milieu* – everyone downing a shot of alcohol halfway through the meal: if it doesn't help things settle, at least it masks the discomfort.

21
Gathering friends for a
Swiss fondue

22 Getting acquainted *with* Arabic sweets

Whenever I go back to Jordan (which is often), my first appointment is in downtown Amman. There, up an unpromising-looking alleyway alongside a bank building, is a hole-in-the-wall outlet of *Habiba*, a citywide chain devoted to *halawiyyat* (literally "sweets", or sweet pastries and desserts). I join a line – there's always a line – and, for the equivalent of a few cents, I get a square of *kunafeh*, hot and dripping with syrup, handed to me on a paper plate with a plastic fork. It is a joyous experience: for the Ammanis hanging out and wolfing down the stuff, it's everyday; for me, it's like coming home. Habiba's *kunafeh* is worth crossing continents for.

Kunafeh is the king of Arabic sweets. Originating from the Palestinian city of Nablus, it comprises buttery shredded filo pastry layered over melted goat's cheese, baked in large, round trays, doused liberally with syrup and cut up into squares for serving. It is cousin to the better-known *baklawa*, layered flaky pastry filled with pistachios, cashews or other nuts, also available widely.

However, you're rarely served such treats in Arabic restaurants: there's not a strong tradition of post-prandial desserts. Instead, you'll need to head to one of the larger outlets of **Habiba**, or their competitors **Jabri** or **Zalatimo**, patisseries with a café section.

Glass-fronted fridges hold individual portions of *Umm Ali*, an Egyptian milk-and-coconut speciality, sprinkled with nuts and cinnamon, and *muhallabiyyeh*, a semi-set almond cream pudding, enhanced with rosewater: comfort food, Arabstyle. Choose one to go with a coffee and perhaps a water-pipe of flavoured tobacco.

Or get a box of assorted sweets – *baklawa*, *maamoul* (buttery, crumbly, rose-scented cookiestyle biscuits), *burma* (nut pastries baked golden brown), *basma* (delicate lacy pastries also filled with cashews) and other delectably sticky and aromatic varieties – the perfect gift if you're lucky enough to be invited to someone's home. Forget, too, about Western-bred inhibitions: in the Arab world, as far as *halawiyyat* are concerned, consumption is guilt-free!

Get on board for a

Keralan sadya

It's hard to imagine a more romantic way to enjoy the extraordinary flavours of India's deep south than drifting across a lagoon just after sunset, against a backdrop of palms, mosque minarets and temple towers.

need to know

Sadya feasts play a central role in the annual Onam harvest festival, held in early September, but rice barge cruises from towns such as **Alappuzha** and **Kollam** serve versions year round.

Aside from the slosh of the oarsman's pole punting you gondolier-style through the shallows, the only sounds likely to accompany your lantern-lit pukka feast – sadya in Malayalam – are the drone of tree frogs and cicadas, and the occasional blast of a Bollywood soundtrack from some village hidden behind the foliage lining the banks.

Sadyas are normally celebratory meals for Christmas or harvest festivals, but you're more likely to encounter them cruising through the Kuttinad backwaters in Kerala. On board, as on land, certain rules dictate the approach. Sadyas are nearly always served on glossy green plantain leaves and eaten with the fingertips. Strict Ayurvedic conventions govern both the placement of dishes and condiments, as well as the combinations of ingredients and spices used.

Once everything is arranged in rows around a central mound of fluffy reddish-white rice, proceedings kick off with a helping of tangy lentil stew called parippu. Next come the main courses, each one with its own distinctive flavour. Depending on the religion or caste of your cook, fish, lamb, clams, or squid may be the prime ingredient. Vegetarian standards – what South India is known for – include *avial* (greens dressed in a creamy coconut sauce), *thoran* (vegetables steamed with grated fresh coconut), various chips (*upperies*) made by deep-frying jackfruit or bananas, and *sambar*, a fiery, watery stew. Coconut and yoghurt temper the incendiary effects of green chilies, while tamarind imparts a subtly sour taste.

Before the leaves are thrown unceremoniously into the water, one final course is whisked out of the kitchen. Prepared from boiled moong beans enriched with cardamom, cashew nuts and cane sugar, *papayasa* is Kerala's best-loved dessert – not least because it soothes the chili burn and promotes sound sleep.

Philly cheesesteak

Ask a native Philadelphian where to go for a proper steak in the City of Brotherly Love, and chances are you won't be shown to the local branch of *Ruth's Chris*. No, in this city where the art museum is best known for a sweaty (and fictional) southpaw fighter lumbering up its storied steps, it's only fitting that you'll be sent to Ninth and Passyunk. At this hardscrabble south Philly corner, **Pat's King of Steaks** and archrival **Geno's** have been grilling Hatfield-and-McCoy-style for the past forty years for the honour of the city's best cheesesteak. It's no small prize – indeed, perhaps no dish in America is as closely tied to a city's mojo.

Join one of the two lines that spill out into the intersection at which these two institutions reside and prepare for fast food nirvana. Ordering requires adhering to a certain local etiquette, specifying first the cheese of your choice – provolone, American or dayglo Cheez Whiz – and then "wit" or "wit-out" to indicate your feelings about grilled onions. It's

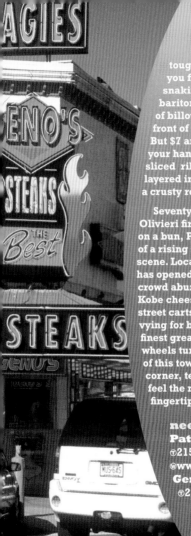

tough not to be a little nervous once you find yourself at the front of the snaking line and a Balboa-esque baritone booms "Next!" from a shroud of billowing steam, before the guy in front of you has even finished his order. But $7 and a "whizwit" later, you've got your hands on a national treasure – finely sliced ribeye grilled hibachi style, layered in gooey cheese and slipped into a crusty roll that's fluffy but firm.

Seventy years after hotdog vendor Pat Olivieri first slapped a slab of grilled steak on a bun, Philly has become something of a rising star on the nation's gourmet scene. Local restaurant guru Stephen Starr has opened a dozen spots to set the Zagat crowd abuzz – even one that hawks a $100 Kobe cheesesteak. But it's the thousands of street carts and unpretentious restaurants vying for bragging rights to the city's finest greasebomb that make Philly's wheels turn. And you won't know the soul of this town until you stand on a street corner, tear off the paper wrapper and feel the molten cheese drip through your fingertips. It's a rite of passage.

need to know
Pat's 1237 E Passyunk Ave
☎215/468-1546,
ⓦwww.patskingofsteaks.com.
Geno's 1219 S Ninth St
☎215/389-0659.

Fish and chips

the true English favourite

need to know

Fish and chips are usually at their best at the seaside, where the fish is freshest. Two noted establishments worth seeking out are **Stein's Fish & Chips**, South Quay, Padstow, Cornwall (☎01841/532700, ⊕www.rickstein.com), and the **Magpie Café**, 14 Pier Rd, Whitby, Yorkshire (☎01947/602058)

Whatever you may think of **fish and chips** – that it's been surpassed as the true English dish by chicken vindaloo, that it's a stodgy recipe for a sure heart attack – there's something undeniably appealing about it. This hot, greasy, starchy mess, smothered with salt and drenched in vinegar, can satisfy like little else.

Quite frankly, you'll probably be served a lot of awful **fish and chips** along the way. This despite the fact that fish and chips is on a bit of roll, even, heaven forbid, nearly fashionable.

All kinds of chefs, buoyed by the renaissance in British cuisine, have been trying their hand at dressing up the humble dish. Indeed, noted gourmet Rick Stein – who has his own **fish and chips** restaurant on the southwest coast in Padstow – has compared serving up a good plate of fish and chips to presenting a plate of Helford oysters with a bottle of *premier cru* Chablis.

Fish and chips has pretty much always meant cod, and it's still far and way the favourite (though now we're told the world is running out), followed by traditional substitutes like skate, plaice, haddock and bottom-feeding rock salmon (the appealing way of saying "catfish" or "dogfish") but gurnard and monkfish are both getting their daring turns in the fryer. As for the batter that invariably coats the fish, flour and water is standard, though you might find yeast and beer batter or matzo meal in the most outré of places. What's the basic chip? Thick cut potatoes, preferably cooked in beef drippings – and of course coated in a light layer of grease and liberal lashings of salt and vinegar.

So maybe that heart attack is coming. Hang the health issues and stuff the cod crisis. Just get stuck in.

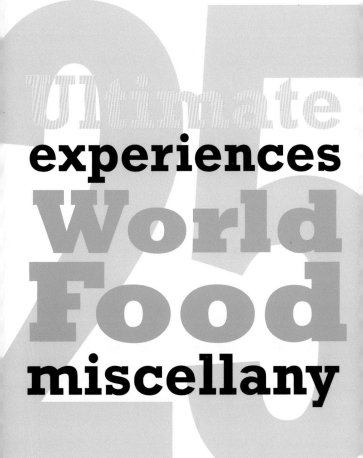

25 Ultimate experiences

World Food

miscellany

1 Dumplings

Dumplings, made from balls of dough or a pastry encasing a tasty filling, are nearly a universal food, with seemingly every ethnicity having their signature variation.

- **pierogi** Boiled or fried Polish-style raviolis stuffed with cheese, potatoes, meat or sauerkraut. Served with a healthy dollop of sour cream.

- **momos** Favoured in Tibet and Nepal, this flour dumpling is filled with vegetables or meat, stacked high and steamed on purpose-built trays.

- **jiaozi** A Chinese dumpling (similar to *gyoza* in Japan) made with minced meat or vegetables and then wrapped into dough, steamed or boiled.

- **samosas** Larger than the other dumplings, the Indian *samosa* is a fried, triangular pastry filled with savoury potatoes, onions and peas.

- **mantu** A Turkish dumpling (closely related to the Asian *mandu*) filled with spiced meat, steamed or boiled, and served with a yogurt and garlic sauce.

2 Table manners

Eating etiquette evolved largely out of practicality, for example "keep your elbows off the table" so that you don't knock anything onto the floor. Unsurprisingly, table manners vary widely according to location (for starters, you may not even be eating at a table).

- **Philippines** Eat whatever is given to you. Food may only be declined in the severest of circumstances – because of an allergic reaction, for example.

- **Afghanistan** If eating at a table and bread is dropped on the floor it should picked up, kissed and put to one's forehead before returning it to the table.

- **Russia** It is considered rude to look into another's plate or cup.

- **China** Never stick chopsticks into a bowl of rice, leaving them standing upwards. This resembles the incense sticks that some Asians use as offerings to deceased family members.

- **Malaysia** Point your feet away from the other guests, lest you be considered impolite.

3 **Dangerous food**

Takifugu (or, colloquially, **fugu**) is a highly toxic pufferfish served as a delicacy in Japan. Because of its poisonous nature, only specially licensed chefs can prepare and sell it to the public, and would-be fugu chefs have to apprentice for two to three years before taking an official fugu-preparation test. Even then, only about one-third of applicants pass the rigorous examination. Ironically, many actually find the fish to be flavourless, eating it solely for the allure of cheating death.

Japanese poet **Yosa Buson** (1716–1783) summed it up with a haiku:

I cannot see her tonight.
I have to give her up
So I will eat fugu.

4 **Diets**

- **Buddhist**   While there aren't universal rules for the Buddhist diet, many monks and nuns choose to abstain from consuming alcohol or meat. In an inverse of Western thinking, Buddhists generally believe it is better karma to feast upon larger animals (such as yak) than smaller animals (such as fish) because the slaughtering of a sizeable animal will provide food for a greater number.

- **Fruitarian**   Participants eat fruit for at least three-quarters of their diet. Some fruitarians only eat what falls (or would fall) from a plant or tree; many are also raw foodists.

- **Kosher**   Diet utilized in the Jewish faith. Forbids consumption of seafood that doesn't have fins or scales, the mixing of dairy and meat products (this is thought to be cooking a calf in its mother's milk) and eating animals that don't "chew their own cud" and have non-cloven hooves.

- **Atkins**   Weight-loss diet at the heart of the low-carbohydrate craze that swept America in the early part of the twenty-first century. Promoted a high-protein, low-carb diet; the Atkins Nutritionals company filed for bankruptcy in 2005.

Five fun food festivals

Event	When and where
Salsa Fair – A celebration of the best in hot sauce – not far from the beach, in case you need to cool off.	Sinaloa, Mexico early May
Taste of Chicago – Said to be the largest food festival. Wonderfully waist-expanding displays of hot dogs, cheesecake and Chicago-style pizza.	Illinois, USA late June through early July
La Tomatina – Visitors and townspeople spend hours mercilessly pegging each other with fistfuls of squashed tomatoes.	Buñol, Spain last Wednesday in August
Oktoberfest – The world's biggest party, with six million attendants. Endless indulging in sausage, sauerkraut and really good beer.	Bavaria, Germany late September
Truffle Festival – Everyone comes to fawn over white truffles – rightfully so – bidding for them at auction and tasting them at markets and restaurants.	Alba, Italy late September to early November

 Edible insects

In much of the Western world, eating insects sounds like a stomach-turning adventure, but that's not true everywhere. Ants are prized in parts of northern Colombia; in South Africa, mopane worms, a species of caterpillar, are popular protein-filled snacks; grasshoppers and bee larvae (*hachinoko*) are enjoyed in some areas of Japan; and in Sardinia, the cheese *casu marzu* is cultivated with the larvae of the cheese fly.

7 Music to eat by

The Cheese Alarm, Robyn Hitchcock. The envelope of silliness gets pushed ("Truckle of cheddar in a muslin rind"), but the sentiment – get this man some cheese, now! – is a winning one.

Pass the Peas, the JBs. A jumping, jazzy, saxophone-driven funk number fronted by James Brown's band in the 1970s. Try their other culinary numbers: "Breakin' Bread" and "Rice 'n' Ribs."

Let's Eat, Nick Lowe. A zingy rave-up about wanting to "move your teeth" and "chew on some meat".

Roast Fish and Cornbread, Lee "Scratch" Perry. Extremely catchy, cryptic reggae tune exalting roast fish and cornbread as "fighting food".

Eggs and Sausage, Tom Waits. His smoky delivery brings you right into the diner booth with him.

Other possibles for a soundtrack include **Know Your Chicken**, Cibo Matto; **Savoy Truffle**, The Beatles; **Cheese and Onions**, The Rutles; **RC Cola and a Moon Pie**, NRBQ; **Ham and Eggs**, A Tribe Called Quest; and, of course, **Escape (The Piña Colada Song)**, Rupert Holmes.

8 Fast facts on fast food

- There are more than 300,000 McDonald's restaurants in 119 countries; McDonald's is located on every continent except Antarctica.
- McDonald's United Kingdom is reputed to use 10.5 million gallons of milkshake and sundae materials yearly.
- Guantánamo is host to Cuba's only McDonald's restaurant, which is located on base and inaccessible to Cubans. Meals from there have been used as rewards for prison detainees.
- The world's most northerly branch of McDonald's is on the Arctic Circle in Rovaniemi, Finland; the most southerly branch is in the city of Punta Arenas, Chile.
- Sälen, Sweden is home to the first McDonald's ski-through.

9 Books

▸▸ Five great food-related books

Fast Food Nation by Eric Schlosser. An eye-opening, entertaining read on the (scary) practices of the fast food industry and its global effects.

North Carolina Barbecue: Flavored by Time by Bob Garner. Well-composed, lovingly researched paean to Southern barbecue. Makes you happy and hungry.

How to Cook a Wolf by MFK Fisher. Wartime manual full of wry humour ("how to be cheerful while starving"), recipes and smart turns-of-phrase from one of the great culinary writers of the twentieth century.

The Kitchen and the Cook by Nicolas Freeling. Eminently readable tales – with some simple recipes thrown in for good measure – about the joys of cooking; the inspiration for *Kitchen Confidential*.

Around the Tuscan Table by Carole Counihan. A readable, not-ultra-romanticized view of Tuscan eating and living put out by a well-known food scholar and ethnographer.

▸▸ Five classic cookbooks that speak for themselves

Essentials of Classic Italian Cooking by Marcella Hazan
Essential Cuisines of Mexico by Diana Kennedy
Mastering the Art of French Cooking by Julia Child
A Taste of Africa by Dorinda Hafner
Thai Food by David Thompson

10 Weird practices

- Icelanders favour a snack of **putrefied shark** (or *hákarl*), reported to taste like cleaning fluid. First-timers generally hold their nose while swallowing the cubed, formerly toxic meat. This is generally followed with a brisk shot of Brennivin, the local firewater.
- **Nyotaimori**, the art of eating sushi off of a naked woman, is a Japanese practice dating back to the late nineteenth century.

Before their shift, servers bathe in fragrance-free soap and splash themselves with cold water to keep body temperature down for the food.

- **Kumis**, or fermented mare's milk, is an important beverage to Mongols and the people of the Central Asian steppes. Kumis production requires great skill – it's tricky to milk a horse – and the beverage is traditionally fermented in a horsehide pouch.
- At the Cooper's **Cheese Rolling** and Wake, participants race downhill after a Double Gloucester cheese wheel, around two feet in diameter; it can reach speeds of 70mph. The winner is rewarded with the cheese.

"Part of the secret of a success in life is to eat what you like and let the food fight it out inside."

Mark Twain

 # Wine

France is the largest wine-producing country in the world, exporting 22 percent of the world's wine sales and producing 5,329,449 tonnes annually. It also is typically said to have the best, holding the renowned regions of Bordeaux, Burgundy and Champagne. Until the latter half of the twentieth century, **American wine** was generally deemed inferior to the European product; it was not until its surprising showing at the Paris wine tasting of 1976 (nicknamed the "Judgement of Paris" in the media) that it commanded worldwide respect.

These five countries lead the world in wine producing:

Country	Signature grape	Characteristic	Best-known regions
Argentina	Malbec	Jammy	Mendoza, Salta
France	Cabernet sauvignon	Tannic, dark fruit	Bordeaux, Burgundy
Italy	Sangiovese	Fruity	Piedmont, Tuscany
Spain	Tempranillo	Earthy	Rioja, Navarra
USA	Zinfandel	Spicy	Napa, Sonoma

12   Movies

▶▶ Five movies that will make you very hungry

Big Night (1996) – Trying to save their old-school Italian restaurant, two brothers cook up a meal highlighted by the serving of a *timpano*, supposedly the mother of all pasta dishes – though not a real dish at all.

Eat Drink Man Woman (1994) – A widowed Taiwanese father's struggles with life and love are revealed via nightly dinners with his adult daughters. Watch it for the tasty food displays as much as for the storyline.

Like Water for Chocolate (1992) – Sensual film set in Mexico about forbidden love, family responsibility and one woman's magical relationship with food.

Babette's Feast (1987) – Set in nineteenth-century Denmark, this arty flick follows two daughters living on the straight and narrow under a devout father. The indulgent feast at its conclusion will make you stand up and cheer.

Tampopo (1985) – Fun, bawdy Japanese film about the opening of a fast-food noodle shop. Billed as the "first Japanese noodle western."

▶▶ Three that may do the opposite

Super Size Me (2004) – An American man documents his bold quest to endure a month of fast food consumption, only eating at McDonald's. Slightly nauseating, yet engrossing.

The Cook, the Thief, His Wife and Her Lover (1989) – Graphic and grotesque allegory, which ends with an eating scene that only the strong will be able to stomach.

Animal House (1978) – John Belushi does his impression of a human zit, proceeded by the best food fight yet caught on film.

13   Chocolate

Few foods come close to matching the allure of chocolate. Consumers spend more than $7 billion a year for a taste of this sweet treat, which reputedly has more than 500 flavour components (more than twice that of strawberry or vanilla). In the US alone, consumers eat 2.8 billion pounds – twelve pounds per person – of the stuff a year.

14 Beer

Said to be the world's oldest alcoholic beverage, beer is best loved in the **Czech Republic**, which annually consumes 159 litres per capita. Essen, **Germany**, has the highest beer consumption of any city in the world with an astonishing 230 litres drunk per person per year. **Belgium** has the greatest number of beer varieties. Beer sales are four times higher than that of wine, the world's second most popular alcoholic beverage. The world's **strongest beer** (recently retired) is Hair of the Dog's *Dave*, a barleywine from Portland, Oregon, with 29 percent alcohol by volume.

15 Taboos

- **Horse meat** is abhorred in the United States as well as the UK, but is common in some parts of continental Europe and is considered a delicacy in Japan (*basashi*).
- The drinking of **blood** is a fairly universal taboo, though the Maasai in Kenya mix cow's blood with milk, and other Kenyans drink camel's blood.
- **Rats** are commonly eaten in Ghana and in rural Thailand, Vietnam and other parts of Indochina.

16 Cheese

Cheese can be made from goat's milk, sheep's milk, cow's milk, yak's milk, even buffalo's, mare's or reindeer's milk. The **US** produces more cheese than **France**, though France exports more of its product – and has many more varieties; Greece consumes the most per capita. England's Cranfield University has claimed in a study that the French cheese Vieux-Bologne is the **stinkiest cheese** in the world.

"How can you govern a country that has 246 varieties of cheese?"

Charles De Gaulle

17 Food origins

Item	What it is	Origin
Pizza	A savoury flatbread traditionally topped with a layer each of tomatoes and cheese.	While pizza's beginnings can be traced to Rome in third century BC, baker Raffaele Esposito of Naples, Italy, is generally credited with making the first modern-day pizza in 1889.
Croissant	Crescent-shaped, buttery French pastry.	Some say it was invented in Poland to celebrate the defeat of a Muslim invasion in 732, others argue that it was invented in Vienna in 1683.
Vegemite	A salty brewer's yeast spread popular in Australia.	Crafted by Fred Walker in Melbourne, Australia (1922); his daughter picked the name out of a hat.
Sushi	Vinegared rice most typically topped with raw fish or other seafood.	While fish was preserved by rice fermentation back in the 1300s, pressing fish and rice into moulds was a cheap meal in eighteenth-century Tokyo.
Hot dog	Sausage-shaped meat blend encased in skin, served in a bun and doused with condiments.	The American hot dog is attributed to the 1904 Louisiana Purchase Exposition in Missouri, USA.

Illicit drinks

Over the years, various alcoholic beverages (often homebrewed) have been outlawed. The most famous of those is **absinthe**; the so-called "green fairy" is a highly alcoholic, anise-flavoured spirit that began in Switzerland and gained popularity for its alleged psychoactive qualities.

Kilju is a traditional Finnish drink, homebrewed with sugar, yeast, fruit or berries and water. Its low cost and few-skills-required fermenting process make it popular among young people and alcoholics; *kilju* made without fruit or berries is considered illegal. **Salep** is a Turkish drink derived from the tubers of various orchid varieties; its popularity has led to the decline of Turkey's wild orchid population, and exporting *salep* is now illegal.

"The superior man does not, even for the space of a single meal, act contrary to virtue."

Confucius

What's for (school) lunch?

- **Israel** Bologna and mayonnaise sandwiches, chicken soup, hummus, schnitzel and potatoes.
- **Japan** Rice cooked with matsutake mushrooms, boiled spinach, fish simmered in soy sauce and rice wine, a light soup and milk. Most main dishes feature rice, but sometimes students eat bread or noodles.
- **France** Iceberg lettuce with radishes and vinaigrette, grilled fish with lemon, stewed carrots, Emmental cheese, apple tart.
- **USA** Pepperoni pizza, French fries, salad bar, chocolate milk.
- **Ukraine** Borscht, sausage or meat cutlet with mash, pancakes or *syrki* with cream cheese.

20 **Stews and soups**

Soup is a universal food and eaten at nearly any time of day (Vietnamese *pho* is a popular breakfast soup, while in China there are plenty of sweet dessert soups, including walnut or red bean). Stews tend to be thicker and more meals in themselves. Here's one recipe for the Sierra Leone version of a hearty West African speciality.

Peanut butter stew

1 pound stewing meat

2 large tomatoes, diced

1/2 cup oil

1/4 cup peanut butter (the less processed, the better – unsweetened is best)

1/2 teaspoon garlic blend seasoning

1 large onion, chopped or sliced

1 large pepper, finely chopped

1/2 teaspoon cayenne, optional

salt to taste

Season meat with garlic blend seasoning. Let it absorb for three hours. Brown meat in oil. Add a dash of water and simmer until tender. Remove and set aside. In the same oil sauté the pepper and onions. Add tomatoes, and stir briskly. Mix peanut butter with 1/2 cup water to form a thin paste and then add to stew. Stir, add meat, salt to taste and let simmer 15 minutes over low heat. Serve with rice, boiled yam, cassava and green vegetables. Enjoy!

21 **Competitive eating**

▶▶ **Six world records you shouldn't try to break**

- Eggs (Sonya Thomas) – 65 hard-boiled eggs in 6 minutes and 40 seconds
- Gyoza (Joey Chestnut) – 212 vegetable and meat gyoza in 10 minutes
- Mayonnaise (Oleg Zhornitskiy) – 4 32oz bowls in 8 minutes
- Meat pies (Boyd Bulot) – 16 6oz meat pies in 10 minutes
- SPAM (Richard LeFavre) – 6lb from the can in 12 minutes
- Hot dogs (Takeru Kobayashi) – 53¾ hot dogs in 12 minutes

22 Size matters

▶▶ The biggest foods ever made

• Omelette (Ontario, Canada) – 6510lbs (2.95 tonnes). Scrambled together by a Canadian-based Lung Association.

• Sandwich (Michigan, USA) – 5440lb (2467.5kg). An American bar and grill beat the previous Mexican record, wherein an enormous ham and cheese sandwich was composed (and eaten) by an audience in Mexico City's Zócalo Square.

• Slab of fudge (Toronto, Canada) – 3010lb (1.36 tonnes). Crafted at an agricultural food fair. Amazingly, nearly every slice was sold.

• Stir-fry (London, England) – 1543lb (700kg). Whipped up by TV chef Nancy Lam to sponsor children's aid charities.

• Tiramisu (Marktheidenfeld, Germany) – 476.1lb (216kg). Composed by chefs at *Café Venezia*, an Italian-based German restaurant.

"Never eat anything that you can't lift."

Miss Piggy

23 Tea

Only water is consumed in greater quantities than tea, but tea's importance tends to go far beyond arguments of whether it's better with milk, lemon or honey, or over ice. On December 16, 1773, in **Boston**, Massachusetts, the first major act of rebellion preceding the Revolutionary War centred on taxed, tea-laden British ships in the Boston Harbour. During the event, one hundred men threw enough British tea into the harbour to make 24 million cuppas.

Tasseography is a method of **fortune-telling** that enables the reader to make predictions from loose tea. The practice originated independently in Asia, the Middle East and ancient Greece, although readers in the Middle East generally favour coffee grounds.

24 Restaurants

The following are reputedly the world's most expensive restaurants (amounts in US dollars):

1. **Aragawa** (Tokyo, Japan): dinner for one $368
2. **Masa** (New York, USA): dinner for one $300
3. **Alain Ducasse au Plaza Athénée** (Paris, France): dinner for one $231
4. **Gordon Ramsay** (London, England): dinner for one $183
5. **Acquarello** (Munich, Germany): dinner for one $125

According to a recent survey, the world's best restaurant is **El Bulli**, near Roses in Spain. The **Fat Duck** in Berkshire, England, and the **French Laundry**, in Yountville, California, are usually mentioned in the same breath.

"After a good dinner one can forgive anybody, even one's own relatives."

Oscar Wilde

25 Cookware and utensils

- **Molcajete** – A traditional Mexican version of the mortar and pestle, made of stone and used for grinding various foods.
- **Chopsticks** – The traditional eating utensil of East Asia (China, Japan, Korea, Vietnam). Legend has it that silver chopsticks were used in the Chinese imperial palace to detect poison (possibly metallic oxides) in the Emperor's meals; if poison was present, the chopsticks would blacken owing to reactions on the silver.
- **Tava** – A large, flat or slightly concave disc-shaped griddle used in Indian cuisine to prepare several kinds of *roti* or Indian breads, including *chapatis* and *parathas*.
- **Forks** – Dubbed the "king of utensils", the fork was introduced in the Middle East around the year 1000; early versions had only two tines.
- **Kushi** – Japanese skewers used to hold and pierce food for grilling and frying, such as yakitori, and are made from steel, bamboo or wood.

25

Ultimate experiences

World Food

small print

ROUGH GUIDES – don't just travel

We hope you've been inspired by the experiences in this book. There are 24 other books in the 25 Ultimate Experiences series, each conceived to whet your appetite for travel and for everything the world has to offer. As well as covering the globe, the 25s series also includes books on **Journeys, Adventure Travel, Places to Stay, Ethical Travel, Wildlife Adventures** and **Wonders of the World**.

When you start planning your trip, Rough Guides' new-look guides, maps and phrasebooks are the ultimate companions. For 25 years we've been refining what makes a good guidebook and we now include more colour photos and more information – on average 50% more pages – than any of our competitors. Just look for the sky-blue spines.

Rough Guides don't just travel – we also believe in getting the most out of life without a passport. Since the publication of the bestselling Rough Guides to **The Internet** and **World Music**, we've brought out a wide range of lively and authoritative guides on everything from **Climate Change** to **Hip-Hop**, from **MySpace** to **Film Noir** and from **The Brain** to **The Rolling Stones**.

Publishing information

Rough Guide 25 Ultimate experiences World Food Published May 2007 by Rough Guides Ltd, 80 Strand, London WC2R 0RL
345 Hudson St, 4th Floor, New York, NY 10014, USA
14 Local Shopping Centre, Panchsheel Park, New Delhi 110017, India
Distributed by the Penguin Group
Penguin Books Ltd,
80 Strand, London WC2R 0RL
Penguin Group (USA)
375 Hudson Street, NY 10014, USA
Penguin Group (Australia)
250 Camberwell Road, Camberwell, Victoria 3124, Australia
Penguin Books Canada Ltd,
10 Alcorn Avenue, Toronto, Ontario, Canada M4V 1E4
Penguin Group (NZ)
67 Apollo Drive, Mairangi Bay, Auckland 1310, New Zealand

Printed in China
© Rough Guides 2007
80pp
A catalogue record for this book is available from the British Library
ISBN: 978-1-84353-836-3

Rough Guide credits

Editor: Andrew Rosenberg
Design & picture research: Andrew Oliver
Cartography: Maxine Repath, Katie Lloyd-Jones

Cover design: Diana Jarvis, Chloë Roberts
Production: Aimee Hampson, Katherine Owers
Proofreader: AnneLise Sorensen

The authors

Zora O'Neill (Experiences 1, 10) writes Rough Guides to the Yucatán and Mexico and has her own food and travel blog, the Roving Gastronome. Roger Norum (Experience 2) writes the Rough Guide to Denmark. Jeff Cranmer (Experiences 3, 24) grew up near Philadelphia, lived in Thailand and writes the Rough Guide to Laos. Martin Dunford (Experience 4, 15) is publishing director of Rough Guides, and writes Rough Guides to Brussels, Rome and Italy. Andrew Rosenberg (Experience 5) is executive editor at Rough Guides and lived on the Lower East Side for years. Mark Ellingham (Experience 6), Rough Guides founder and series editor, writes the Rough Guide to Morocco. Brendon Griffin (Experience 7) contributes to the Rough Guide to Spain. Stephen Keeling (Experience 8) writes the Rough Guide to Taiwan. Rosalba O'Brien (Experience 9) contributes to the Rough Guide to Argentina. Donald Reid (Experience 11) writes Rough Guides to Scotland and the Scottish Highlands & Islands. Jan Dodd (Experience 12, 17, 20) writes Rough Guides to Dordogne & the Lot, Vietnam, and Japan. David Leffman (Experience 13) co-authors the Rough Guide to China. Richard Trillo (Experience 14) is co-author of the Rough Guide to West Africa. Oliver Marshall (Experience 16) is co-author of the Rough Guide to Brazil. Dave Dakota (Experience 18) has eaten oysters in more than twenty countries. Samantha Cook (Experience 19) writes Rough Guides to New Orleans and the USA. Matthew Teller (Experiences 21, 22) writes Rough Guides to Switzerland and

Jordan. **David Abram** (Experience 23) is co-author of the Rough Guide to India. **Robert Andrews** (Experience 25) is co-author of the Rough Guide to England. **Sarah Hull** (Miscellany) loves Tibetan momos as much as Maine lobster, though may prefer vegemite to both.

Picture credits

Cover Woman eating rice, Guizhou Province © Nancy Brown/Getty Images

2 Tajine © Marko MacPherson/Getty Images

6 Night market in Taipei © Jean Marc Truche

8–9 Maryland crabs © iStockphoto

10–11 Swedish breakfast buffet © Bo Zaunders

12–13 Food prep in Thailand © Thomas Holton

14–15 Pizza-making © Borchi Massimo/Four corners Images (both images)

16–17 Bagel with lox and cream cheese © Roy Morsch/Corbis

18–19 Tajine © Marko MacPherson/Getty Images

20–21 Chef Juan Mari Arzak © Jean Dominque Dallet/Alamy; Tapas bar in San Sebastián © TNT Magazine/Alamy; San Sebastián restaurant menu © Sandra Baker/Alamy; Pinxtos © Toni Vilches/Alamy

22–23 Night market in Taipei © Jean Marc Truche; Food stand in Taipei © MIXA Co Ltd/Alamy; Skewered barbecue squid © Henry Westheim Photography; Sesame ball © MIXA Co. Ltd

24–25 Argentinean parilla © Axiom; Cowboy and cattle © Axiom; Barbecued meat © Axiom

26–27 Tacos © Look Die Bildagentur der

28–29 Loch Eriboll in northern Scotland © Imagebroker/Alamy; Whisky nosers examining flavour and colour © South West Images Scotia

30–31 Sarlat, France © Jon Arnold Images/Alamy; Garlic bulbs © Cristina Fumi; Red peppers at market stall in Sarlat © Simon Cross Travel Images/Alamy; Sarlat market © Huw Jones/Alamy;; Lemons at market stall in Sarlat

© Simon Cross Travel Images; Local produce in Sarlat © Images-of-France/Alamy

32–33 Hanging roast ducks © Ludwig M Brinckmann/Alamy

34–35 Nyama choma bar in Kenya © Peter Horree/Alamy

36–37 Belgian chocolates © Ken Welsh/Alamy; Chocolate shop in Belgium © Alamy

38–39 Academia da Cachaça, Rio de Janeiro © Ricardo Beliel/BrazilPhoto/Alamy; Caipirinhas © Stockfood

40–41 Kaiseki-ryori food © Pacific Press Service/Alamy

42–43 Moored boats © Per Breiehagen; Oyster vendor © Getty Images

44–45 Galatoire's, in New Orleans' French Quarter © Rough Guides; Coffeemaking in Galatoire's © Alamy

46–47 Snake wine © Jon Arnold Images/Alamy; Snake restaurant, Hanoi © Terry Whittaker/Alamy (two images)

48–49 Fondue © Stockfood

50–51 Sweets vendor © IML Image Group LTD; Typical Arabic sweets in Amman © Jochen Tack/Alamy; Kunafeh pastry © Shutterstock; Arabic sweet © Barry Mason/Alamy; Pile of baklawa © Eddie Gerald/Alamy

52–53 Keralan sadya © Axiom; Fishermen in Kerala © Neil Emmerson

54–55 Philly cheesesteak © brt FOOD/Alamy; Philadelphia © Andre Jenny/Alamy

56–57 Fish and chips © Sparky; Eating chips by the seaside © Pick and Mix Images/Alamy

58 Pile of baklawa © Eddie Gerald/Alamy

Fly Less – Stay Longer!

Rough Guides believes in the good that travel does, but we are deeply aware of the impact of fuel emissions on climate change. We recommend taking fewer trips and staying for longer. If you can avoid travelling by air, please use an alternative, especially for journeys of under 1000km/600miles. And always offset your travel at www.roughguides.com/climatechange.

Over 70 reference books and hundreds of travel
guides, maps & phrasebooks that cover the world

ROUGH GUIDES

ROUGH GUIDES

ROUGH GUIDES

ROUGH GUIDES

ROUGH GUIDES

ROUGH GUIDES

RO GU

Australia

Cuba

Britain

Singapore

Vietnam

New York City

Index